SERIAL KILLER TED BUNDY

BUNDY

Dr. V.V.L.N. Sastry

Table of Contents

About the Book

Bundy's criminal behavior as a serial killer can be explained in terms of Freud's psychological theory. According to Freud, a person's behavior comes about because of interactions between three aspects of his or her personality including the superego, ego, and id. Id drives instinct and controls what a person does from birth. There are both constructive and destructive instinctual drives. A person's ego moderates his or her instinctual drive while the superego is needed for a person's development during which he or she learns the values of society. As Freud puts it, large portions of ego and superego can remain unconscious, making an individual unaware of whatever he or she is doing (Ahmed, 2012). Examples of unconscious experiences include disturbing memories and extreme sexual behaviors. If the person becomes aware of these unconscious experiences, he or she is likely to engage in destructive behavior. It can be concluded that Bundy's ego and superego may have been unconscious when he was committing initial criminal activities. However, when his awareness was restored, he responded by even more destructive behavior like when he decided to kidnap and kill more than one lady during the day (Ahmed, 2012). This book analyses the serial killer Ted Bundy.

About the Author

Graduate in Technology, Dr.V.V.L.N.Sastry. Sastry, holds  M.B.A, LL.M, ACMA (India), FCMA (CIMA, UK), M.Sc in Information Systems and Management from University of Roehampton, Ph.D in Banking, Ph.D in Computer Science, Ph. D in Financial Management, and Ph.D in Criminal Law and Public Policy from Walden University, U.S.A. Sastry, brings over 20 years of experience in the banking, investment banking, software industry and law. He is the author of more than 1000 published articles on varied subjects in the areas of IT, Banking, Finance, Economics and Law. He also has authored several books in the said fields. Rated among the top researchers in the worldwide applied academics by www.academia.edu, his applied research contributions are well received across the world.

Dr. V.V.L.N. Sastry

Detailed Overview

Ted Bundy, initially known as Theodore Robert Cowell is one of the most famous serial killers in the United States. The motivation for this paper is to understand the potential social, environmental, biological, genetic, and psychological factors that contributed to Bundy's criminal behaviors. Born in 1946, Ted Bundy grew up without knowing the identity of his father. During his early years, Ted Bundy's mother took him to her parents who he later thought to be her real parents. In order to drive away the shame, Bundy's mother made him understand that she was actually his older sister. Bundy was an obedient and respectful child who also performed well in school. He even qualified to join University where he pursued a degree course in psychology and eventually law. It is during his university life when Ted Bundy fell in love with a young lady for the first time. Unfortunately, they broke up, and Bundy was highly devastated. Just a few months after the break-up, Bundy discovered that his older sister and parents were actually his mother and grandparents respectively (Pedneault, 2002).

Bundy was a serial killer who continuously assaulted and brutally murdered young women. He committed serial murders in the Washington State, Utah, Colorado, Idaho, and Florida before his arrest. The first assault committed by Bundy was confirmed on January 4th, 1974 when he entered the bedroom of a female dancer and student aged 18 years. Bundy sexually assaulted the girl before beating her with a metal rod. This lady was from the University of Washington. Although the girl did not die from the beating, her brain was permanently damaged. In the same month, Bundy killed another female student from the University of Washington before dumping her body in a separate location. Two months later, he kidnapped and murdered another female student aged 19 years. Bundy's next attack was in April 1974 when he lured and killed another lady from Central Washington State College. He later killed two more university female students in the months of May and June 1974 (Pedneault, 2002).

In July the same year, Bandy changed his tactics for committing crime from abducting female students during the night to kidnapping them during the day. On the same day, Bundy abducted and murdered two ladies by luring them to help him unload some luggage from his Volkswagen Beetle. The two females were from Washington State's Lake Sammamish State Park. Following all these murders in the Washington State, police officers began to hunt for a criminal they had very little information about. They distributed Ted Bundy's sketches and descriptions to television and newspaper stations. Bundy's girlfriend, Ann Rule, later reported to the police that Ted Bundy was a possible suspect. However, they ignored the report due to the fact that Bundy was a law student (Pedneault, 2002).

Dr. V.V.L.N. Sastry

Towards the end of 1974, Ted relocated to Utah to continue with his studies in Salt Lake City. While in Utah, Bundy continued to kill young females, this time, not university students. He managed to capture his victims by pretending that he was a police officer conducting a criminal investigation. Unfortunately, Bundy did not succeed in all his murder attempts because two ladies escaped before they were killed. This did not discourage him, he went on to kill another female student aged 17 years when she was going to pick her brother from school. After killing several ladies in Utah, Bundy decided to target ladies from Colorado and Idaho because he had been spotted by Utah residents. He killed four separate ladies in Colorado and Idaho between January and May 1975 (Pedneault, 2002).

Bundy was arrested in 1975 in Utah when he failed to stop for a police check. Police searched his car and they found burglary tools such handcuffs, a crowbar, and a ski mask. His car was linked to the other murders and abductions in Utah making the police officers to treat his case as that of murder. He was convicted of murder in March 1976, but he later escaped in 1977. After six days, Bundy was brought back to jail where he escaped again seven months later. This time, Bundy moved to Florida where he attacked four female university students in January 1978 and later killed another one in February the same year. He was arrested less than a week later before he was executed on January 24th 1989. Bundy confessed to have assaulted and murdered 35 young ladies (Pedneault, 2002).

Bundy's criminal offending is consistent with what is known about the nature of serial killers. According to Rippo (2007), serial killers are always confident that they will never be arrested. Additionally, a serial killer often believes that he can outsmart the police and they do not express fear of whatever they do. Similarly, Bundy was confident that he will never be apprehended. This is evident in the manner he used his real names when introducing himself to victims. Furthermore, Bundy exposed his identities to people in authority because he knew that police officers will never catch up with him. Bundy also loved being noticed everywhere he went. Although Ted managed to escape during his early days of criminal activities, he was completely not aware that his girl friend, Ann Rule had set him up (Rippo, 2007).

Causes of Crime

The potential social and environmental causes of Bundy's behavior

Socialization is one of the most important environmental factors that shape a child's behavior. Levy and Orlans (2004) defines socialization as the way a child interacts with others and does things. A child often learns by observing what people in his or her immediate surrounding are doing. During this stage of childhood development, a child gets to know different rules and values of the society. When certain actions are repeated, the child internalizes them and even tries to apply them as he or she continues to grow. The type of behavior developed by a child is determined by the actions observed in his or her environment. This explains why it is important to teach a child to internalize morally and socially acceptable behaviors at the right time to prevent him or her from developing antisocial behaviors in future. As Levy and Orlans (2004) point out, if a child is taught to exhibit certain characteristics, he will believe that they are inherently correct. Therefore, a child who is not taught to exhibit the right behaviors is very likely to develop criminal behaviors.

Bundy was brought up with his mother alone and he grew up without his father's identity. Even though Bundy's birth certificate stated that he was the son of an Air force veteran who later married his mother, it is suspected that Bundy's must have given fathered by Louise's abusive and violent husband (Michaud and Aynesworth, 1999). Since Bundy was only a teenager, his mother referred to him as her brother in order to avoid embarrassments. Even though Bundy's mother was always there for him during childhood, she failed to provide him with social and emotional support. Basically, there was no close relationship between Ted and his mother which interfered with his social development. Perhaps, this had a great impact in building Bundy's serial killer characteristics. According to Michaud and Aynesworth (1999), a child who fails to secure parental love during childhood is likely to experience a wide range of problems such as behavioral and social problems, which may lead to development of anti-social behavior. The fact that Bundy grew up without a father figure may have affected his ability to develop positive social behaviors.

In addition, Bundy grew up in a childhood marked with poverty despite the fact that his mother and grandparents tried their best to provide him with whatever he needed. Throughout his high school and college life, Bundy remained a loner, which made him shy even as he interacted with his school-mates (Leibman, 1989). According to Leibman, (1989), poverty has a direct connection with offensive behaviors and juveniles who grow up in poverty are at high risk of developing criminal behaviors. When in college, Bundy felt isolated and

Dr. V.V.L.N. Sastry

uncomfortable among his rich and wealthy peers, leading to his transfer to the University of Washington (Leibman, 1989).

Lack of good social relationships during childhood prevented Bundy from understanding the importance of interpersonal relationships during adulthood. For this reason, Bundy had no problems presenting a false social image to people around him. When Bund met his first girlfriend in college, he loved her so much that he was ready to do all that he could to please her. After one year, the relationship broke up after Bundy's girlfriend realized that he was not the right man for her. This break-up affected Bundy emotionally, even contributing to him dropping out of school. These frustrations, coupled with childhood feelings, Bundy decided to quit college after which he moved to the countryside. Bundy began to kill young women shortly after he was rejected by his girlfriend. According to Leibman (1989), serial killers

Dr. V.V.L.N. Sastry

often begin to kill as a result of increasing frustrations, rejection, and anger. Bundy began to develop characteristics of a serial killer as a result of increasing frustrations which was experiencing. He developed a negative attitude towards young women, which acted as the main reason why he engaged in violent behaviors.

Bundy's hatred towards young women increased even further when he decided to go back to college where he fell in love with another woman. He could not tell the lady the truth about his life because he feared that the lady might leave him. After dating for three months, Bundy and his girlfriend planned to get married but he later changed his mind that it was too soon. Ideally, it is Bundy's past life experiences which prevented him from getting into serious relationship with another lady. Bundy and his girlfriend continued to go out until one day he forced her to have anal sex with him leading to their break-up. After graduating from Washington University, Bundy decided to continue his relationship with the first girlfriend but the relationship ended a few months later (Rule, 2000). Consequently, Bundy ended up with nobody to share his social life with, not even his mother. This may have contributed greatly to his antisocial behavior in Washington State, Utah, Colorado, Idaho, and Florida.

In Bundy's case, his family contributed greatly to his development of criminal behavior while his girlfriends made him develop hatred towards young females. According to Levy and Orlans (2004), poor parenting practices such a parent's rejection of a child is a predictor of future delinquency by a child. Family influences are greater than other social factors when it comes to shaping of a child's behavior during the period of childhood development. Poor parental supervision during a child's teenage life has also been identified as a contributing factor for future offending. Bundy's serial killer characteristics could not have been developed if he could have received maximum parental love and support (Levy and Orlans, 2004).

The potential psychological causes of Bundy's behavior

It is often difficult to specify the psychological factors that contribute to a criminal behavior. However, psychological influence on a person's criminal behavior can be determined by analyzing the effect of individual and family factors on offending. In order to correctly associate certain psychological factors with offending, one must be able to study a person's life over time. In Bundy's case, the psychological factors that influenced the development of serial killer characteristics can be determined by looking at his life from childhood to adulthood. According to Farrrington (2013), offending is just one element of antisocial behaviors which develop after a person has experienced several psychological problems.

One of the psychological theories used to explain the development of criminal behaviors is attachment theory that focuses on the nature of relationship between a child and his parents or with people close to him. In Bundy's life, there was loss of attachment with his parents for a total of three years which prevented him from forming meaningful relationships. Isolation and lack of affection made Bundy to have poor impulse control coupled with chronic anger (Bowlby, 1969). When Bundy was living with his grandparents whom he knew as his parents, he used his grandfather as his role model. Bundy's grandfather took time to teach him good morals which were aimed at making him a well-behaved person in the society in future. Unfortunately, Bundy's mother separated him from his grandparents at the age of four when she relocated to Washington. Bundy developed fear of separation or loss which made him to begin developing violent behaviors while in Washington. According to Bartol and Bartol (2011), separation from loved ones can generate strong feelings of anxiety in a person, often leading into violent behaviors. Even though Bundy did not share any bond with his parents, he decided to react to the separation by becoming angry (Leibman, 1989). Bundy suffered depression when his grandmother failed to take care of some of his childhood needs. This early depression and anxiety prevented Bundy from forming meaningful relationships with his peers during childhood, which damaged him both neurologically and psychologically. He later found out that being a serial killer is the best way through which he could respond to the psychological torture that he was experiencing (Leibman, 1989).

According to Farrrington (2013) illegitimacy is a paramount psychological factor that is likely to affect a child's moral life. The impact of illegitimacy may be severe to an extent that it may prevent a child from leading a normal life. Majority of parents who give birth to children and later choose to live as single parents normally put a huge burden on the child. For instance, if a single parent decides to enter into a new marriage, he or she may prevent the child from enjoying parental love. This is because the new parent will not have a balanced loving attitude to his or her illegitimate child. This may end up affecting the child both emotionally and psychologically. The child may develop a feeling of inferiority which may prevent his or her future achievements. As a way of reacting to life's failures, the child may engage in criminal activities in their future in life (Farrrington, 2013).

After relocating to Washington, Bundy's mother got married to another man and as a result, his name was changed to avoid future embarrassments by strangers. At the age of six years, his mother gave birth to another child, followed by other three which made Bundy to feel even more isolated. To make matters worse, Bundy was informed that his mother's husband was not his real father. It is during this time that he also learnt that his mother was not actually his sister and that his 'parents' were actually his grandparents. This ignited Bundy's anger after learning that he had been kept in the dark for more than ten years.

His mother however continued to go for picnics and many other trips with his step-father and siblings while he was kept distant. All these placed Bundy at a high risk of developing violent and anti-social behaviors. According to Whitman and Akutagawa (2004), a child who is neglected by the mother will engage in behaviors that can assist him or her to gain a sense of control such as masturbation and other sexual fantasies.

Bundy's criminal behavior as a serial killer can be explained in terms of Freud's psychological theory. According to Freud, a person's behavior comes about as a result of interactions between three aspects of his or her personality including the superego, ego, and id. Id drive instinct and it controls what a person does from birth. There are both constructive and destructive instinctual drives. A person's ego moderates his or her instinctual drive while the superego is needed for a person's development during which he or she learns the values of

Dr. V.V.L.N. Sastry

society. As Freud puts it, large portions of ego and superego can remain unconscious, making an individual unaware of whatever he or she is doing (Ahmed, 2012). Examples of unconscious experiences include disturbing memories and extreme sexual behaviors. If the person becomes aware of these unconscious experiences, he or she is likely to engage in destructive behavior. It can be concluded that Bundy's ego and superego may have been unconscious when he was committing initial criminal activities. However, when his awareness was restored, he responded by even more destructive behavior like when he decided to kidnap and kill more than one lady during the day (Ahmed, 2012).

The potential biological and genetic causes of Bundy's behavior

Different researchers have documented that antisocial behavior has a biological and genetic basis. Initial investigations carried out on twins revealed that antisocial behavior can be inherited from parents, and this may present in various forms of aggression and criminality. Additionally, majority of personality factors exhibited by criminals such as risk-taking and impulsivity are genetically influenced (Baker, Bezdjian and Raine, 2006). According to Baker, Bezdjian and Raine (2006), genes can be a very strong predictor of whether a person strays into a life of crime. This is because genes can make a person to become a persistent offender, with antisocial characteristics being developed right from childhood through adulthood.

There is clear evidence that genetics may have played a big role in the development to Bundy's criminal behaviors. According to Shapiro (2005), Bundy's grandfather was a very violent person. Bundy could observe him beat the family dog and swung neighborhood cats by their tails. Since Bundy witnesses his grandfather's violent behaviors when he was still a child, these behaviors might have influenced the learning of violence towards animals and people around him. One could say that Bundy inherited the violent behaviors from his father. Apart from the violent behaviors, Bundy also exhibited very disturbing and strange behaviors unlike those of his peers. One day, his grandmother woke up and found kitchen knives placed all around her. She was surprised to see Bundy smile at her. Such things cannot be done by someone who lacks genes associated with violent and disturbing behaviors (Leibman, 1989).

Criminal behaviors influenced by genetic factors take time to manifest especially due to change in the life conditions that a person lives in. According to Baker, Bezdjian and Raine (2006), heritability varies according to ages with certain antisocial behaviors being manifested more during childhood than adulthood and others being manifested more during adulthood than childhood. In Bundy's case, his criminal behaviors were manifested more during adulthood than during childhood. For instance, he did not commit homicide until when he was in his early 20s. His serial killer characteristics were influenced greatly at this age by the pornographic and terrifying movies that he watched. Bundy spent most of his time watching pornographic movies and magazines filled with dead and mutilated bodies. This influenced him to move around in the neighborhood searching for bare windows that revealed young women undressing. Bundy confessed that once he became addicted to such kinds of behaviors, he took his time searching for additional materials with very explicit pictures. Comprehensive analysis of Bundy's criminal records reveal that he committed limited crimes during childhood but Rule (2009) documents that he was arrested twice when he was in high school for theft and burglary.

Although several studies reveal that genetics have a direct influence on antisocial behavior, some researchers have found out that genetics has an indirect influence in traits that predict occurrence of an antisocial behavior. Examples of these traits include impulsivity and attention deficit. According to Baker, Bezdjian and Raine (2006), people exhibit different antisocial behaviors due to variations in their personality characteristics such as impulsivity. These traits are also heritable indicating that genes modulate behaviors that involve impulse control. Bundy's serial killer characteristics may have developed as result of inheritance of personality characteristics from his father.

Apart from genetics, other biological factors such as neuro-biology and neuro-transmitters could have a great impact on development of Bundy's serial killer characteristics. Many studies have found that there is a close link between antisocial personality disorders and specific crimes that involve impulsivity. This is because impulsivity is also influenced by neuro-transmitters. The structure and function of the brain is what is referred to as neuro-biology. When the structure and function of the brain is analyzed through magnetic resonance imaging, there is increasing evidence that neurological damage greatly influences offending (Baker, Bezdjian and Raine, 2006). For instance, damage to the frontal cortex through head injury is highly linked to antisocial behavior. Aggressive feelings have been found to result from pre-frontal damage. This explains why the early years of a child's development require close attention from the parent. Negative experiences during childhood development may cause neurological deficit in a child which may lead to criminality during adulthood. The physical abuse and neglect that Bundy experienced during childhood might have cause neurological deficits which later predisposed him to criminality (Leibman, 1989).

Another thing that is believed to have influenced Bundy's serial killer characteristics is the fact that he felt genetically sophisticated than his stepfather. Bundy felt that he was a child of a father whose identity he did not know and he related his status with financial and social problems he was experiencing. This feeling of genetic difference forced Bundy to steal other people's belongings, with his main targets being young women who had rejected him sometimes in life. Additionally, Bundy was biologically inferior in the sense that, he was shy and incapable of forming strong relationships with his peers. This resulted into isolation which contributed greatly to development of serial killer characteristics (Leibman, 1989).

Type of Offender

Ted Bundy was a serial killer who repeatedly abducted and murdered young women both at night and during the day. Carbajal (2010), defines a serial killer as a person who repeatedly attacks and murders his or her victims in a number of incidents. Serial killers normally kill different innocent people for their personal satisfaction and they use strange methods to lure or capture their victims. There are different types of serial killers and they are categorized base on their motives of killing. For instance, a visionary serial killer is normally instructed by some voices to kill his or her victims. Missionary serial killers normally feel that they have a responsibility of getting rid of a certain group of people from the world. Another group of serial killers is lust killers who are normally attracted to kill due to sexual motivation. Thrill killers often murder their victims because they enjoy the experience of killing. Bundy was a lust killer who

Dr. V.V.L.N. Sastry

murdered his victims as a result of sexual motivation (Carbajal, 2010).

Ted Bundy possessed the unique characteristics presented by serial killers. According to Rippo (2007), approximately 89 percent of known serial killers are Caucasian males aged between 25 and 35 years. The IQ of serial killers often ranges from 105 to 120 or even more. For instance, Ted Bundy had an IQ of 140 which demonstrated that he was a highly intelligent serial killer. Some serial killers normally target a particular group of victims. In such a case, the objective of the serial killer is to eliminate the kind of group it is targeting. Ted Bundy only targeted young women as a way of expressing his anger and hatred towards this particular group of people. Majority of killers who murder their victims due to sexual motivation do so because they have some sort of sexual bondage. When Ted Bundy was interviewed, he stated that he was attracted to kidnap and kill young females because he was strongly addicted to pornography (Carbajal, 2010).

According to Carbajal (2010), many serial killers come from dysfunctional families where parents are either divorced or where parents completely abandoned their children. In most cases where parents are together, either of the parents may not express love for the child. Additionally, serial killers are known to have suffered either physical or sexual abuse at one time in life. Ted Bundy came from a dysfunctional family with his parents having separated when he was still very young. When his mother got married to the military man, Bundy did not receive parental love from his step-father and he even suffered depression because of neglect. Moreover, Bundy had suffered both sexual and physical abuse during his early years. All these factors contributed greatly to Bundy being a serial killer (Rippo, 2007).

Majority of serial killers are known to suffer from Antisocial Personality Disorder. People suffering from Antisocial Personality Disorder are known to exhibit good intelligence, impulsiveness, insincerity, and lack of guilt. Ted Bundy's criminal activities were largely inclined to boredom and enjoyment, as well as impulsiveness. This demonstrates that he might have been suffering from Antisocial Personality Disorder. A high percentage of Bundy's victims were middle aged female college students. However, these characteristics differed at times depending on his choice of victims. Bundy was described as charismatic based on the way he used intelligence to win the confidence of his victims. Occasionally, Bundy revisited the crime scene grooming and performing sexual acts with corpses until they completely decayed. This gave him an opportunity to take full control of his victims' bodies both when they were alive and they were dead (Carbajal, 2010).

Historically, many serial killers have committed very horrible crimes by killing innocent people and torturing animals. Serial killers share a number of personality traits with most traits being observed during childhood. Some of these traits include abusing animals, bet wetting, and setting fires on properties. All serial killers are motivated to kill in different ways and they are driven to kill by various factors. Whatever the reason, serial killers have destroyed many innocent lives whether or not their actions are influenced by social, environmental, psychological, genetic, and biological factors (Carbajal, 2010).

The fact that the actions of serial killers are normally influenced by different factors makes it difficult for these types of offenders to be rehabilitated. As initially mentioned, there are different types of serial killers with other murdering their victims due to sexual motivation, finances, and for fun. Roberts, Zgoba and Shahidullah

(2007), conducted a study to find out whether there is any possibility that a serial killer can be rehabilitated. He found out that there is no correlation between reductions in rates of serial killing following rehabilitation. From this study, it was concluded that serial killers are difficult to rehabilitate due to variations in their motives and ideologies. Even though majority of serial killers share common traits during childhood, their developmental stages are always different leading to acquisition of new traits that are unique to individuals. For instance, some serial killers may experience brain injuries as they continue to grow which may influence their serial killing characteristics during childhood (Roberts, Zgoba and Shahidullah, 2007). Conversely, some people argue that serial killers can be rehabilitated so long as the contributing factors are effectively identified and the correct treatment offered to help drive away their intentions of committing murder. According to BBC News (2009), serial killers can be rehabilitated to an extent that they are able to return to the outside world and blend well with other members of the society.

Apprehension

As a serial killer continues with his profession, he normally believes that a serial he cannot be apprehended. For this reason, majority of serial killers make a mistake of leaving behind their identification that can be used by police officers to apprehend them (Rippo, 2007). For instance, Ted Bundy used to introduce himself to his victims using his real names. Throughout his life, Bundy was confident that there is not any given time when police officers will ever catch up with him. For years, police officers have conducted investigations by scrutinizing everything that might have been used by the offender including clothes, masks, guns, tissue papers, among others. They even go to an extent of matching DNA to genetic chromosomes contained in fluid samples obtained from the serial killer suspects. These criminal profiling strategies have assisted police officers to apprehend the

Dr. V.V.L.N. Sastry

exact serial killers. Similarly, criminal profiling could be used to apprehend Ted Bundy even sooner (Rippo, 2007).

According to Rippo (2007), criminal profiling is only applicable to extremely violent homicide cases such as serial killing. When criminal profiling is used, it assists the profiler to easily narrow down his or her search of the serial killer. Even though there are various things to consider when conducting criminal profiling, the profiler will always focus on the crime scene and the specific types of victims targeted by the offender. Apart from narrowing the offender, criminal profiling will help the profiler to lower the number of victims. Information that the profiler will be obtained from the profile will be used to identify the specific victims which will help to apprehend the offender faster. For instance, criminal profiling can be used to identify the specific victims affected by Ted Bundy's criminal behaviors, especially those who managed to escape. This information can be used to track Bundy bearing in mind that he introduced himself to his victims using his real names (Rippo, 2007).

Criminal profilers have been trained to handle crimes of different types. For instance, profilers are able to investigate and apprehend all types of serial killers so long as they can identify their motives for killing their victims. The criminal profiler uses deductive reasoning to investigate the crime scene and search for the serial killer. Through deductive reasoning, it could have been easier for the profilers to relate Bundy's behaviors to the crime scenes. According to Rippo (2007), criminal profiling is a powerful tool for searching a serial killer because it helps to speed up investigations. Although it is not the work of the profiler to apprehend the criminal, the information that he or she produces is very useful for the criminal justice system.

In Bundy's case, criminal proofing could have assisted the profiler to eliminate other suspects who were associated with the crimes he had committed. This is because the information that the profiler could have obtained from the profile could be used for a more specific search for the offender (Rippo, 2007). Additionally, by understanding the type of offender that Bundy is through the profile, the profiler becomes properly equipped during the interrogation process. This is because the interrogation techniques applied when conducting a criminal investigation are based on the personality characteristics of the offender. Since the main goal of criminal profiling is to assist the law enforcement officers with their investigations, it is clear that Bundy could have been apprehended sooner through criminal profiling (Rippo, 2007).

Information obtained from profiling Bundy can be very useful in the apprehension of future criminals. After Ted Bundy was interviewed by criminal profilers, the information obtained assisted investigators to understand what goes on in the mind of a serial killer. For example, the criminal profiler found out that all Bundy's victims were young White females aged between 15 and 25 years. This information can be used to locate serial killers after finding out whether they target a particular group of victims. Additionally, Bundy drank alcohol before he could move out to hunt for his victims. This means that a serial killer normally has a specific thing that he or she must do before committing crime. Law enforcement officers can easily apprehend serial killers in future by finding out whether they like engaging in certain behaviors before they can commit murder (Rippo, 2007).

Moreover, almost all Bundy's victims had been strangled to death. This information can be used by law enforcement officers to apprehend serial killers in future by identifying the methods of murder used by offenders. Again, after luring his victims, Bundy incapacitated his victims by hitting their heads using a crowbar and other blunt objects (Rippo, 2007). Future serial killers can be apprehended by finding out whether they used blunt objects to incapacitate their victims before killing them. The details obtained from Bundy's profiling can be used to arrest serial killers because this type of offenders have been found to have several characteristics in common irrespective of the nature of the environments in which they have developed (Rippo, 2007).

Policy Implications

The death of Bundy revived the debate over capital punishment with other supporting it while others fighting for its abolition. One question that one needs to ask himself is why all nations that are fighting for a free society have abolished capital punishment except the United States. In 1960s, majority of Americans opposed capital punishment, but is surprising that currently, more than two thirds of the population is supporting it. By supporting capital punishment, the society tends to express its anger by depriving the killer of his or her life. Yet, a free society should be concerned with respecting the right of all its citizens. With reference to Bundy's case, some people argue that capital punishment should be abolished because it does not make sense when a society kills murders in order to teach them that killing is a crime. For instance, the criminal justice system did not help Bundy at all by allowing him to undergo a death sentence because he was a serial killer (Greenfield, 1989).

Instead of using capital punishment, the United States should use severe forms of punishment that will enable the wrong door to recognize that whatever the crime he or she committed was wrong. In Ted Bundy's case, he was subjected to capital punishment yet he did not kill while stealing his victims' property. This shows how much the nation does not value the lives of its citizens. If a person wants to judge whether a given country is oppressive or free, he or she should find out whether it imposes a death penalty on serial killers or murderers. According to Greenfield (1989), the main reason why a country should oppose capital punishment is due to the fact that, nobody should have power over a person's life. If a government disobeys the rights of its citizens, it is regarding itself as the judge of whether a person should live or should die. From the Bundy's crimes and from his death, nations can now learn to formulate policies that do away with capital punishment.

Policies that support capital punishment should be replaced by those that will encourage prevention of crimes such as those committed by Bundy. For example, the national government should come up with laws that will ensure that all children are placed under care of a responsible adult even if such children are orphans. Such a policy will help prevent young children from developing criminal behaviors, especially those behaviors that are influenced by environmental, social, biological, genetic, and psychological factors. Additionally, the national government should formulate policies that will ensure that all criminals in the society are provided with the best form of rehabilitation. Policies that support rehabilitation must be effective enough to ensure that all criminals in the society develop positive behaviors (Greenfield, 1989).

References

Ahmed, S. (2012). *Sigmund Freud's psychoanalytic theory Oedipus complex: A critical study with reference to D. H. Lawrence's "Sons and Lovers."* Retrieved from http://www.academicjournals.org/article/article137 9514083_Ahmed.pdf

Baker, L. A., Bezdjian, S., & Raine, A. (2006). Behavioral genetics: The science of antisocial behavior. *Law Contemporary Problems 69*(1-2): 7-46.

Bartol, C. R., & Bartol, A. M. (2011). *Criminal Behaviour: A Psychological Approach.* Upper Saddle River, New Jersey: Pearson.

BBC News. (2009). *Can serial killers be rehabilitated?* Feb. 20, 2009. Retrieved from http://news.bbc.co.uk/2/hi/uk/7899143.stm

Bowlby, J. (1969). *Attachment and loss: Volume 1. Attachment.* New York: Basic Books.

Carbajal, K. (2010). Dr Hannibal "The Cannibal" Lecter and Serial Killers: Does abuse beget violence? *The science of fiction: Evolutionary explanations of hypothetical human behaviour volume 2.* California, LA: University of California.

Farrrington, D. P. (2013). *Crime causation: Psychological theories-Family influences, individual influences, more comprehensive theories, conclusions, biography.* Retrieved from http://law.jrank.org/pages/813/Crime-Causation-Psychological-Theories.html

Greenfield, J. (1989). *Bundy revives the death penalty debate executions tell about a nation.* Retrieved from http://articles.philly.com/1989-01-

26/news/26123262_1_penalty-executions-capital-
punishment

Leibman, F.H. (1989). Serial Murderers: Four Case
Histories. *Federal Probation 53*(4), p.41 – 44.

Levy, T., & Orlans, M. (2004). Attachment Disorder,
Antisocial Personality and Violence. *Annals of the
American Psychotherapy Association 7*(4), p. 18.

Michaud, S., & Aynesworth, H. (1999). *The Only Living
Witness: The True Story of Serial Sex Killer Ted
Bundy*. Irving, Texas: Authorlink Press.

Pedneault, A. (2002). *Ted Bundy on the "malignant
being": An analysis of the justificatory discourse of
a serial killer*. Retrieved from
http://www.sfu.ca/~palys/crim862-Pedneault-
TedBundyJustificatoryDiscourse.pdf

Rippo, B. M. (2007). *The professional serial killer and the
career of Ted Bundy: An investigation into the*

macabre identity of the serial killer. United States of America: iUniverse

Roberts, A. R., Zgoba, K., & Shahidullah. (2007). Recidivism among four types of homicide offenders: An exploratory analysis of 336 homicide offenders in New Jersey. *Aggression and Violent Behavior* 12: 493-507.

Rule, A. (2009). *The Stranger Beside Me*. (Paperback; updated 2009 ed.) NY: Signet

Rule, A. (2000). *The Stranger Beside Me*. (Paperback; updated 20th anniversary ed.) NY: Signet

Shapiro, B. (2005). *Porn Generation*. Washington, DC: Regnery Publishing.

Whitman, T. A ., & Akutagawa. (2004). Riddles in serial murder: A synthesis. *Aggression and violent behaviour 9*(6), p. 693-703.